CW01082942

Original title:
The Creator's Path

Editor: Theodor Taimla
Author: Paul Pääsuke
ISBN HARDBACK: 978-9916-87-006-8
ISBN PAPERBACK: 978-9916-87-007-5

Stirrings in the Realm of Dreams

In the hush of night, whispers call,
Shadows dance where night falls.
Stars twinkle like distant eyes,
In the realm where silence sighs.

Clouds of thought drift and roam,
Weaving worlds that feel like home.
Fleeting moments, soft and bright,
Guide the wanderer through the night.

Visions swirl in swirling mists,
Echoes of forgotten trysts.
Dreamers chase what hearts desire,
As spirits twirl in cosmic fire.

Fragments of life weave through air,
Drifting on dreams, free of care.
Time pauses, breaths hang still,
As wishes ride on moonbeam's thrill.

Awakening brings a gentle sigh,
Hope nestled beneath the sky.
For in dreams, there lies a spark,
Igniting journeys from the dark.

Mosaics of Inspiration

Fragments of colors, vibrant and bright,
Each piece a story of hope and light.
Together they form a vision so grand,
A tapestry woven by nature's hand.

In shadows and whispers, dreams come alive,
A dance of the heart where passions thrive.
Each tile a moment, a memory dear,
Crafting a mosaic that conquers fear.

Sculpting the Unseen Realities

From whispers soft, a vision grows,
In shadows deep, the artist knows.
With gentle hands, they mold the clay,
Crafting realms where hearts can play.

Each stroke paints a world anew,
Textures sparkle in every hue.
Imagination soars and flies,
As unseen truths begin to rise.

Chiseling dreams from silence deep,
Awakening thoughts from ancient sleep.
Moments captured in time's embrace,
Reflect the beauty of the human race.

A tapestry of hope and light,
Woven together in the night.
With every curve and every line,
The unseen dances, pure and divine.

Reality bends in gentle sway,
As visions merge with night and day.
Through crafted paths, we make our way,
In unseen realms, forever stay.

Thus, we dream and thus, we mold,
Creating tales yet to be told.
In the sculptor's heart, truth ignites,
Illuminating the darkest nights.

Mosaics of Inspiration

Fragments of colors, vibrant and bright,
Each piece a story of hope and light.
Together they form a vision so grand,
A tapestry woven by nature's hand.

In shadows and whispers, dreams come alive,
A dance of the heart where passions thrive.
Each tile a moment, a memory dear,
Crafting a mosaic that conquers fear.

Sculpting the Unseen Realities

From whispers soft, a vision grows,
In shadows deep, the artist knows.
With gentle hands, they mold the clay,
Crafting realms where hearts can play.

Each stroke paints a world anew,
Textures sparkle in every hue.
Imagination soars and flies,
As unseen truths begin to rise.

Chiseling dreams from silence deep,
Awakening thoughts from ancient sleep.
Moments captured in time's embrace,
Reflect the beauty of the human race.

A tapestry of hope and light,
Woven together in the night.
With every curve and every line,
The unseen dances, pure and divine.

Reality bends in gentle sway,
As visions merge with night and day.
Through crafted paths, we make our way,
In unseen realms, forever stay.

Thus, we dream and thus, we mold,
Creating tales yet to be told.
In the sculptor's heart, truth ignites,
Illuminating the darkest nights.

Echoes of Divine Design

In silence we hear the heavens call,
Whispers of grace through the echoing hall.
Stars paint the sky with celestial ink,
Inviting the soul to step back and think.

Nature reflects a divine hand in play,
Guiding us gently through night and day.
Life's gentle rhythm, a sacred refrain,
Each moment a note in the grandest gain.

Visionary Trails

Steps on the paths, in twilight's glow,
Visionaries wander, seeds to sow.
With each stride, new ideas arise,
In the forest of thoughts, wisdom lies.

Through valleys low and peaks so high,
Chasing dreams that touch the sky.
A heartbeat pulses, future in sight,
Along these trails, we find our light.

Sketching futures with every turn,
In each silence, lessons to learn.
The spirit guides through winds of change,
In visionary trails, hearts rearrange.

Bridges built on hopes and fears,
Navigating through laughter and tears.
With every step, a story unfolds,
In the visionary echoes, love holds.

Mapping dreams, till paths align,
Together we rise, our spirits entwine.
In the embrace of vast skies, we sail,
Carving our legacy on visionary trails.

Tapestry of Envisioned Realities

Threads intertwine in a dreamer's loom,
Crafting a vision to banish the gloom.
Colors and textures in harmony blend,
A tapestry woven from start to end.

Futures unwrapped in the fabric we weave,
A dance of belief that we freely conceive.
Each stitch a promise, each weave a world,
A canvas of hope patiently unfurled.

Canvas of Life

Brushstrokes of time, colors blend,
Moments captured, whispers send.
Each layer tells a tale profound,
In the quiet, dreams are found.

Framing joys, shadows cast,
Every hue a memory vast.
Canvas stretches, endless space,
Life's portrait in a graceful trace.

Threads of hope, a tapestry,
Woven with fragility.
The artist's heart beats in the strokes,
In silent voices, beauty provokes.

Seasons change, the palette shifts,
In every corner, nature lifts.
A canvas born from tears and laughter,
Life's masterpiece, forever after.

Underneath the starry night,
Colors gleam, a pure delight.
On this canvas, we unfold,
Stories painted, bright and bold.

Footprints on the Canvas

Impressions we leave upon life's spread,
Marking our journeys with dreams unsaid.
Each step a brushstroke on time's open face,
Creating a picture of love and grace.

With colors and shadows, we leave our mark,
In delicate silence and loudest spark.
Footprints of courage, of joy, and of pain,
A canvas reflecting the storms and the rain.

Dancer Among Ideas

Twisting thoughts, a ballet bright,
Ideas swirl in the soft moonlight.
Each step crafted, elegant flow,
In this dance, wisdom will grow.

Spinning dreams, they take their flight,
Among the stars, pure delight.
Rhythms pulse, the mind's embrace,
Imagination finds its space.

A leap of faith, spontaneity,
In every turn, possibility.
With every sway, new realms ignite,
A dancer thrives in the twilight.

Echoes whisper, secrets share,
In the silence, wonder's flare.
Dance of thoughts, a vibrant spree,
Freedom blooms in creativity.

Boundless moves, the heart takes lead,
In this dance, we plant a seed.
Among ideas, we find our grace,
Dancer swaying in time and space.

Footprints on the Canvas

Impressions we leave upon life's spread,
Marking our journeys with dreams unsaid.
Each step a brushstroke on time's open face,
Creating a picture of love and grace.

With colors and shadows, we leave our mark,
In delicate silence and loudest spark.
Footprints of courage, of joy, and of pain,
A canvas reflecting the storms and the rain.

Dancer Among Ideas

Twisting thoughts, a ballet bright,
Ideas swirl in the soft moonlight.
Each step crafted, elegant flow,
In this dance, wisdom will grow.

Spinning dreams, they take their flight,
Among the stars, pure delight.
Rhythms pulse, the mind's embrace,
Imagination finds its space.

A leap of faith, spontaneity,
In every turn, possibility.
With every sway, new realms ignite,
A dancer thrives in the twilight.

Echoes whisper, secrets share,
In the silence, wonder's flare.
Dance of thoughts, a vibrant spree,
Freedom blooms in creativity.

Boundless moves, the heart takes lead,
In this dance, we plant a seed.
Among ideas, we find our grace,
Dancer swaying in time and space.

Map of Infinite Journeys

Lines etched on a weathered page,
Adventures await, set the stage.
Paths intertwine in mystic ways,
Where the heart leads, time obeys.

Mountains high and valleys deep,
Every journey, a promise to keep.
Rivers flow, the compass spins,
In every turn, excitement begins.

Stars align in the endless night,
Guiding dreams toward the light.
Every road a tale to tell,
In exploring, we find ourselves well.

Footsteps echo, a quest begun,
Chasing shadows, capturing fun.
Explore the map, let spirit soar,
Each journey is an open door.

Endless horizons call my name,
With every venture, we're never the same.
In this map, the world is wide,
A canvas for hearts and hopes to bide.

Pulses of the Divine Fabric

In the quiet hum of night,
Stars weave their soft embrace,
Whispers of time take flight,
Shimmering in sacred space.

Threads of love intertwined,
Nature's rhythm, a grace,
Hearts aligned and minds,
Dancing in the cosmic chase.

Each pulse a heartbeat's song,
Echoing through the divine,
In unity we belong,
A tapestry, all entwined.

Fading shadows, light ignites,
Glimmers of hope arise,
Carving paths through endless nights,
Underneath the vast black skies.

Infinite dreams unfurl,
Guided by an unseen hand,
In the fabric of the world,
Together we take our stand.

Creating with Cosmic Threads

With every breath, we create,
Mysteries of the vast unknown,
Crafting wonders that await,
In the ether, seeds are sown.

Galaxies begin to spin,
Dreams woven with every strand,
In the silence, we begin,
To mold our future, hand in hand.

Colors burst and hues collide,
In the canvas of the night,
Imagination as our guide,
Igniting the dark with light.

Threads of fate we intertwine,
Crafting realms from thought and prayer,
In the universe, we shine,
Creating worlds beyond compare.

From stardust, stories arise,
Weaving tales of love and truth,
In this cosmic paradise,
We find the wisdom of our youth.

The Unwritten Manuscript

Pages blank, yet filled with dreams,
Stories linger in the air,
Ink of fate flows in gentle streams,
Awaiting hands that truly care.

Each chapter waits to be defined,
Voices echo through the void,
In our hearts, the words aligned,
A melody that won't be snubbed.

Time will shape the pen's embrace,
Guiding thoughts through winding prose,
In the quiet, we find grace,
As imagination freely flows.

The climax hides in whispered lines,
A hero's journey yet to come,
Through valleys deep, the heart finds signs,
Each moment, a story's drum.

As the pages turn, we yearn,
For every twist and every bend,
In our souls, the meaning burns,
Unwritten tales will never end.

Voyage through Transcendence

Set sail on a sea of light,
Waves of wisdom pulling near,
In the mist, we find our sight,
Journeying beyond all fear.

Stars our compass, souls the map,
With every heartbeat, we ascend,
In this vast celestial lap,
We discover where worlds blend.

Current carries us through time,
Moments folding, futures free,
In the rhythm, life's sweet rhyme,
As we drift in harmony.

Awake to realms of the divine,
Every breath a sacred prayer,
In this voyage, pure and fine,
Love will guide us everywhere.

Through the cosmos, we explore,
Boundless spirits intertwining,
In this dance, forevermore,
Transcendence through stars, shining.

Wandering Through the Infinite

In shadows deep the wanderer roams,
Through endless paths and ancient homes.
Stars whisper secrets in the night,
While dreams take form in silver light.

Each step reveals a hidden truth,
In the echo's call of forgotten youth.
Galaxies spin in silent grace,
Time bends softly, a warm embrace.

Waves of stardust kiss the ground,
In every silence, a heartbeat found.
Misty trails of fate collide,
In the tapestry where worlds abide.

Lost in wonder, found in flight,
Embracing all, both dark and bright.
Each moment leads to endless skies,
In wandering hearts, the universe lies.

Embers of the Soul's Journey

Through ashes deep, the fire glows,
Where silent strength within me grows.
Each ember whispers tales of old,
Of dreams ignited, hearts turned gold.

In shadows cast by flickering flame,
I search for meaning, call my name.
With every breath, the spark ignites,
Guiding my path through endless nights.

Cinders dance in the stillness rare,
Casting warmth in the midnight air.
I gather courage from the light,
Awakening hope in the heart of night.

From whispered winds on distant shores,
To lifetimes lived behind closed doors.
Each journey shapes the soul I bear,
In the embers, I find solace there.

Notes from the Cosmic Tuner

A symphony plays in the midnight sky,
Notes that shimmer as they fly.
Galactic rhythms pulse and sway,
In harmony's embrace, we drift away.

The cosmic tuner strums the strings,
Of stars and dreams, of ancient things.
Melodies weave through the silent seas,
Carried softly on the breeze.

With each vibration, worlds align,
Echoes of life in hearts divine.
In every whisper, a promise found,
In the celestial dance, we spin around.

Through blackened voids and glowing light,
We find our song, our inner sight.
Let the universe guide the tune,
In the cosmic ballet, we are in bloom.

The Heart's Altar

Upon the altar, my heart does lay,
Offering dreams with no words to say.
In silence deep, the truth unfolds,
As whispered secrets dare to be bold.

With every beat, a prayer ascends,
A quest for love that never ends.
Fragments of joy and sorrow blend,
In the sacred space where spirits mend.

Candles flicker in the depth of night,
Casting shadows that dance in light.
Here lies hope, a sacred trust,
In the heart's altar, pure and just.

Through trials faced and battles fought,
I gather wisdom, lessons sought.
In gratitude, I bow and see,
The heart's altar, my soul set free.

Flickers of the Divine Mind

In the quiet night, sparks begin,
Thoughts take flight, the dance within.
Visions shimmer, soft and bright,
Guiding hearts through shadowed light.

In the stillness, whispers flow,
Beneath the stars, secrets glow.
Ideas bloom, like flowers rare,
In the silence, love found there.

Fragments of dreams weave and wend,
From the soul, where dreams ascend.
Each flicker hints, a truth refined,
A glimpse of grace, the divine mind.

In this moment, all can see,
Infinite paths, a tapestry.
With every breath, a spark ignites,
Illuminating endless nights.

Catch the echoes, feel the grace,
In the heart, our sacred space.
Together we forge, hand in hand,
Flickers of the divine planned.

Crafting Worlds from Silence

In the hush, a spark takes form,
Silent whispers, a quiet storm.
Words unspoken, visions cast,
In the still, the die is tossed.

From shadows deep, realms arise,
Imagination learns to fly.
Each thought a thread, woven tight,
Crafting worlds from silent night.

Boundless skies where dreams collide,
In the void, we learn to ride.
Empty spaces, filled with grace,
Silence births a sacred place.

With every pause, new realms expand,
An architect with gentle hand.
Creating life from quiet calls,
Crafting worlds, where spirit sprawls.

Through stillness, we uncover truth,
Lost in the echoes of our youth.
Each moment, a canvas wide,
Crafting dreams where hearts reside.

Harmonies of the Infinite

In the cosmos, chords resound,
Melodies wrap the earth around.
Stars collide, in rhythmic dance,
Creating magic, giving chance.

Softening edges, every note,
In the stillness, we will float.
Unified in a heartbeat's pulse,
Harmonies blend, dissolving sulks.

Time unwinds in perfect flow,
Infinite realms where feelings grow.
With each breath, a sound so sweet,
The universe, a soft heartbeat.

Together we sing, souls combined,
Tuning hearts to the divine.
Every echo, pure and bold,
In harmonies yet to be told.

Journey forth, where light aligns,
Through the darkness, a path shines.
In this melody, we find our way,
Harmonies guide, as night meets day.

Blooming Futures

In the garden, seeds take root,
Dreams held close, a tender shoot.
Nurtured by hope, sun, and rain,
Blooming futures rise again.

With every blossom, stories born,
Potential waits in every thorn.
Fragile petals, strong and bright,
A testament to hope and light.

Time will shape what we believe,
In the warmth of love, we cleave.
Through the struggle, we find grace,
Blooming futures, our shared space.

Colors spark in radiant swirls,
Painting visions, future pearls.
Every heart can cultivate,
A garden rich with hope and fate.

In the springtime of our dreams,
Life awakens, bursting seams.
Together we plant, hand in hand,
Blooming futures across the land.

Unfolding the Unwritten

Pages whisper tales untold,
In shadows where secrets unfold.
Ink flows like a river's grace,
Carving futures in time and space.

Brave hearts seek the path anew,
In every dawn, a chance to pursue.
Dreams dance on the edge of night,
Illuminating the void with light.

The quill trembles, ready to write,
Adventures born in the still of night.
Each word a breath, alive and clear,
A symphony of hopes we hold dear.

In silence, we gather the stars,
Mapping the heavens, counting the scars.
Faith ignites in the ink's embrace,
Unfolding stories in sacred space.

With every verse, a journey begun,
Woven together, woven as one.
The unwritten awaits our hand,
To shape the dreams of this vast land.

Crucible of Dreams

In the furnace where passions ignite,
Dreams are forged in the depths of night.
Molten hopes, a shimmering blend,
Transforming fears as they bend.

Each heartbeat a pulse in the dark,
Where visions emerge, igniting a spark.
The weight of clouds, heavy with rain,
Yet through the storm, we find our gain.

Winds of change whisper and sway,
Guiding footsteps along the way.
In the crucible's fierce embrace,
We find our strength, we find our place.

With hands calloused from shaping the clay,
We carve our futures, come what may.
In the heartbeat of hope, we arise,
Crafting our fate beneath endless skies.

When shadows linger, dreams stand tall,
In the belly of the beast, we sprawl.
Forged in fire, our spirits soar,
In the crucible of dreams, we explore.

Palettes of Potential

Colors blend on nature's canvas,
Each stroke a wish, each hue a promise.
Brushes dance with vibrant glee,
Painting futures for you and me.

In the quiet of dawn, hues awake,
Shades of dreams in every quake.
The palette whispers, full of grace,
Inviting us to find our place.

Splashes of courage, dabs of fear,
Creating a masterpiece, crystal clear.
With every heartbeat, a story unfolds,
In the colors of life, our truth beholds.

Beneath the skies, free we roam,
Crafting visions, making them home.
Each blend a memory, vivid and bright,
Painting our journey, day and night.

In the gallery of dreams we reside,
Where potential flows like an endless tide.
With every brush, we redefine,
In palettes of potential, we shine.

Handprints of Time

On the canvas of history, we leave our marks,
Imprints of laughter, whispers, and sparks.
Each handprint a tale in the sands of the past,
Reminders of moments, both fleeting and vast.

Time dances lightly on fragile skin,
Every touch a story, the where and the when.
Silhouettes of love echo through years,
Each gesture a passage through joy and tears.

From cradle to dusk, our journey unfolds,
Handprints of wisdom, both daring and bold.
In every heartbeat, the rhythm does chime,
Eternal connections—our handprints of time.

As seasons change, we grow and we learn,
Through trials we weather, in passion we burn.
Carving legacies with each loving sign,
We shape our existence, our handprints align.

In the dance of the stars, we find our place,
Threads woven together in time's warm embrace.
A tapestry rich with experiences sublime,
Forever we linger in handprints of time.

Tapestry of Intent

Threads of purpose intertwine,
Crafting dreams within the loom.
Colors whisper, soft and fine,
Woven visions find their room.

Fingers dance on fabric's heart,
Each stitch speaks of hope anew.
Designs emerge, a work of art,
Guided by a steady view.

In the warmth of sunlight's grace,
Patterns shift with every breath.
Gentle hands embrace the space,
Life unfolds beyond the depth.

Threads may fray but never break,
Strength lies in each woven tale.
Every choice a path we make,
Intent echoes, swift as sail.

So we weave, each dream a thread,
In the tapestry of the night.
Boundless visions lie ahead,
In the fabric, we find light.

Journey of Illumination

Step by step, we walk the trail,
Guided by the starry glow.
In the silence, whispers sail,
Carrying the truths we know.

Each encounter lights the way,
Flickering in the darkened skies.
Through the night, we find our play,
In the dreams where wisdom lies.

Mountains rise, and rivers wind,
Nature speaks in vibrant hues.
In the heart, all paths aligned,
Journey brings us brighter views.

Shadows stretch, but fear won't win,
Hope ignites with every breath.
Through the fire, we begin,
To create from life's sweet depth.

With each dawn, we rise and shine,
Brighter than the day before.
In the heart, our spirits twine,
Journey leads us evermore.

Essence of Imagination

In the mind, worlds come alive,
Colors dance and shapes take flight.
Thoughts can bloom, and dreams can thrive,
In the realm of hidden light.

Castles rise from grains of sand,
Skies painted in hues of gold.
In this space, we take a stand,
Every story waiting to be told.

Whimsical paths twist and turn,
Chasing echoes of the heart.
In the silence, passions burn,
Imagination plays its part.

Time unwinds in gentle streams,
Every spark ignites a flame.
From our souls, we weave our dreams,
In this dance, we find our name.

So let thoughts take wing and soar,
Into realms both wide and vast.
In the heart, forevermore,
Imagination holds us fast.

Chronicles of the Artisan

Hands of skill, a tale unfolds,
Crafting beauty from the earth.
In each piece, a story told,
Wrought from passion, love, and mirth.

Chisel strikes and brushstrokes fly,
Every detail, a labor of heart.
With each moment, spirits rise,
Artisans play their timeless part.

Clay meets hand, smooth forms arise,
Metal sings beneath the flame.
In the eyes, a spark defies,
Creation's wild and boundless game.

Through the years, their hands endure,
Marking time with steadfast grace.
In each craft, a heart so pure,
Leaving whispers in this space.

So we gather, tales entwined,
In each piece, a touch of soul.
Chronicles of life defined,
Artisans make the world whole.

Seedlings of Ingenuity

In quiet soil, dreams take root,
Gentle whispers, truth's pursuit.
A spark ignites in fertile ground,
Where silent hope and growth abound.

With every leaf that reaches high,
Inventive thoughts begin to fly.
A tapestry of visions bright,
Crafting worlds from day to night.

Each seedling blooms with vibrant grace,
A testament to time and space.
From humble starts, the bold arise,
Wings of ambition touch the skies.

Through winter's chill and summer's glow,
Ingenuity begins to flow.
Beneath the stars, our plans align,
A garden rich with dreams divine.

With every breeze, we're carried forth,
To chase the dreams that hold us north.
In unity, our spirits sing,
The seedlings dance, and hopes take wing.

Paths of Possibility

Footsteps tread on winding trails,
Where wonder stirs and courage prevails.
Beneath the shades of ancient trees,
A symphony of whispered pleas.

Each fork reveals a choice to make,
A leap of faith, or stay awake.
In every turn, a story spun,
Endless journeys just begun.

With every step, horizons blend,
Boundless roads that twist and bend.
Together we embrace the chance,
To weave our dreams in vibrant dance.

Through valleys deep and mountains high,
The spirit soars, the heart will fly.
With every path that we embrace,
The map becomes a sacred space.

As dawn breaks forth, new light ignites,
Guiding us through wondrous sights.
In unity, we carve our way,
On paths of possibility each day.

Lightbearer's Voyage

Upon the sea where stars align,
A vessel sails through realms divine.
The moon bestows a silver sheen,
Guiding dreams to realms unseen.

With each wave that breaks and swells,
The heart of adventure gently tells.
An odyssey of souls combined,
In search of treasures yet defined.

The compass spins with visions bright,
A tapestry of hope and light.
With every breath, the journey calls,
Through tempest storms and tranquil halls.

As gentle winds the sails do fill,
A lightbearer before the thrill.
Their spirit shines, a beacon true,
Leading the way for me and you.

In twilight's embrace, the anchor falls,
And echoes dance through silent halls.
Together, we shall find our shore,
In light's warm glow, forevermore.

Emissary of Imagination

In realms where dreams and visions meet,
An emissary stirs a world, discreet.
With painted thoughts that leap and twirl,
A symphony of dreams unfurl.

The canvas waits for colors bold,
As whispers of creation unfold.
With every stroke, the story breathes,
As magic weaves through time and leaves.

Through portals wide, imagination flies,
To sketch the clouds, to paint the skies.
A dance of wonder in the air,
A tapestry beyond compare.

In shadows deep and brightened light,
The emissary brings forth new sight.
From fragile dreams, a vision grows,
In every heartbeat, beauty flows.

Together we embrace this chase,
To grasp the wonders, make our place.
In dreams we trust, our spirits free,
Imagination's boundless tapestry.

Illuminating Forgotten Paths

In shadows deep, where silence dwells,
Whispers find their ancient spells,
Footsteps trace the tales of old,
In dreams awake, the stories unfold.

A lantern's glow, a gentle flame,
Guides the wanderer, calls their name,
Through tangled woods and winding ways,
The heart ignites a path that sways.

Over hills where echoes stray,
Memories linger, soft as clay,
Carved in stone, a fragile time,
The pulse of life, a rhythmic rhyme.

Each twist and turn, a lesson gained,
A tapestry of joy and pain,
Illuminating paths once lost,
A journey rich, no matter the cost.

With open hearts, we tread anew,
Embracing what we thought we knew,
Each forgotten trail, a chance to see,
The beauty in our history.

Seeds of Creation in Full Bloom

From tiny seeds in fertile ground,
The world awakens, life profound,
Petals stretch and colors rise,
A symphony beneath the skies.

Gentle rains and warming sun,
Nurture dreams, each one begun,
In every bud, potential swells,
In whispers soft, creation dwells.

Nature's canvas, bold and bright,
Brushstrokes dance in pure delight,
Every hue a story spun,
In blooming fields, our hearts are won.

The breeze carries the scents of change,
While rhythms of the season range,
Hope takes root in tender grace,
In every flower, a sacred space.

Together, we watch the garden thrive,
In blooms of passion, we arrive,
Seeds of creation, bursting free,
In every heart, our legacy.

The Poet's Hearth

In the quiet glow of midnight's fire,
Words take flight, hearts conspire,
A dance of shadows, whispers spun,
In the stillness, all is one.

Ink drips softly, stories flow,
From barren thoughts, ideas grow,
Every line a piece of soul,
Within the warmth, we become whole.

The flicker of flames, a guiding light,
Crafts our dreams in the night,
Each stanza a chamber of the heart,
Building bridges, creating art.

As ember fades and dawn unfolds,
The poet's heart eternally holds,
Fragments of life in tender verse,
In every blessing, every curse.

From hearth to heart, a bond so dear,
In vulnerability, we persevere,
The stories told, a timeless start,
In every poem, we share our heart.

Blueprints of the Heart

Within the chambers, whispers beat,
Blueprints drawn in love's retreat,
Each sinew woven, hopes align,
In fragile strength, designs divine.

Lines of laughter, scars of pain,
The architecture of our gain,
Walls built strong from dreams we share,
Embracing all the truths we bear.

In twilight's glow, the sketches gleam,
A symphony of hopes and dreams,
Together, we construct the scheme,
And find our place within the theme.

Through storms and trials, the heart withstands,
With every heartbeat, love expands,
In the blueprints, life takes part,
As we draw closer, heart to heart.

With every breath, foundations grow,
Creating spaces where love can flow,
In this design, we find our place,
Blueprints of the heart, woven with grace.

Navigating the Nebula of Ideas

In a vast expanse, thoughts collide,
Colors swirling, hopes untied.
Stars of wisdom flicker bright,
Guiding paths through endless night.

Each spark ignites the heart's desire,
Carving dreams that never tire.
Lost in cosmic thoughts, we roam,
Finding truth, we build a home.

Galaxies of visions unfold,
Whispers of stories yet untold.
Through the void, our spirits dance,
In the labyrinth, we take a chance.

Nebulas form, we shape our fate,
Embracing change, we cultivate.
In every hue, a chance to grow,
Navigating where ideas flow.

As we traverse this grand expanse,
We learn to lead, we learn to dance.
Through the stars, our passions soar,
Navigating the timeless lore.

The Alchemy of Vision

In the crucible of dreams, we blend,
Ideas crystallize, messages send.
Turning shadows into light,
In our grasp, we hold the night.

Elixirs brewed from lost despair,
Transforming visions, bold and rare.
Every thought, a precious gold,
In this alchemy, we are bold.

Crafted gently with hands of care,
Breath of wisdom fills the air.
Through the lens of heart's embrace,
We find our path, we find our place.

With each drop, we mold the clay,
Shaping futures in a fray.
Alchemy of vision calls,
In our hearts, a spirit sprawls.

Each potion mixed, a story spun,
In the tapestry, we are one.
Creating worlds from what's unseen,
The alchemy flows, vibrant and keen.

Brushstrokes of Destiny

With a steady hand, the painter moves,
Crafting life, where passion grooves.
Colors splash on canvas wide,
In each stroke, our dreams abide.

Every hue, a tale to tell,
In the silence, we weave our spell.
Shadows dance with vibrant light,
Defining contours, day and night.

The brush whispers secrets rare,
Of hopes fulfilled and deep despair.
Through the swirls, our hearts ignite,
In creation's grasp, we find our right.

Brushstrokes weave through time and space,
Embodying fleeting moments' grace.
In every hue, our destinies lie,
A masterpiece beneath the sky.

As the palette bridges gaps,
We find our voice, escaping traps.
With each finish, a new story flows,
Brushstrokes of destiny, forever glows.

Chasing Light in Shadowed Realms

In the twilight where shadows play,
Hope emerges, guiding the way.
Footsteps echo, soft and clear,
Chasing dreams without a fear.

Through the darkness, courage shines,
Flickering like hopeful signs.
In the depths, we seek the light,
Finding strength to face the night.

Whispers of dawn awaken souls,
Breaking through the world's black holes.
With every step, the journey stirs,
Chasing light, the spirit purrs.

In the realms where shadows dwell,
We find the magic in the spell.
Boundless, wild, we run and fly,
Chasing dreams beneath the sky.

Light and shadow intertwine,
Creating paths that feel divine.
In every heart, a flicker gleams,
Chasing light, we live our dreams.

Wanderer of Dreams

In the still of night I roam,
Through the shadows of my mind,
Where the heart finds peace and home,
And the lost are often kind.

Stars above like secrets gleam,
Guiding me through the unknown,
Each step woven like a dream,
In the dark, I am not alone.

Whispers float on silken air,
Every sigh a tale to tell,
In this realm, I shed my care,
Riding waves of memory's swell.

With each thought, I chase the light,
Painting hues of hope anew,
In the silence of the night,
I find colors deep and true.

Nature's pulse becomes my guide,
Every heartbeat sings of grace,
In this world where dreams abide,
I embrace the endless space.

Sculptor of Stars

Underneath the endless drift,
Where the cosmos speaks in glow,
I will carve with gentle gift,
Chasing echoes to and fro.

Galaxies dance in my hands,
Constellations form and fade,
With the softness of the sands,
I create the paths they laid.

Light and shadow intertwine,
Every twinkle starts to breathe,
In the dark, the fates align,
As I mold what we believe.

Sculpting realms of vast expanse,
With the whispers of the night,
Every star a timeless chance,
To ignite the hidden light.

In this boundless dreamscape space,
I am both the clay and hand,
Forge a universe with grace,
Crafting wonders, bold and grand.

Echoes of Inspiration

In the silence, voices rise,
Whispers borne on gentle breeze,
Every note a sweet surprise,
Carried forth with perfect ease.

Moments spark like sunlit rays,
Painting thoughts with vibrant hue,
In the labyrinth of days,
I find paths that feel so true.

Echoes dance in hidden places,
Nestled deep in heart and soul,
Each reflection softly traces,
What it means to feel whole.

In the heart of all creation,
Dreams resound like distant chimes,
Marking every single station,
Through the tapestry of times.

With each breath, I dare to reach,
For the spark that lights the mind,
Every thought a lesson teach,
In the echoes, joy I find.

Weaver of Whispers

Threads of silk in twilight loom,
With each strand, a story goes,
In the quiet, end of gloom,
Weaving tales that softly flows.

Every whisper holds a song,
Gentle as a lover's kiss,
Binding us where we belong,
With the threads of what we miss.

In the fabric of the night,
Stars entwined in whispered threads,
Bringing forth a hidden light,
Where the path of hope still spreads.

Woven dreams, so rich and rare,
In the loom of fate's embrace,
Every thought a work of care,
In the silence, find your place.

Weaving whispers, hearts conjoin,
With each stitch, a sacred pact,
In the tapestry, we join,
Together, ever intact.

Whispers of the Artisan

In quiet rooms where shadows play,
The artisan weaves dreams in clay.
Fingers dance with grace and care,
Echoes of beauty linger in the air.

With every stroke, a story born,
Sculpted visions, gently worn.
Colors blend in soft embrace,
Crafting moments, capturing grace.

As sunlight warms the polished floor,
Art from silence begins to soar.
Whispers of passion fill the space,
Imprints of joy in every trace.

From rough edges, forms arise,
Mirroring the ancient skies.
An artist's heart beats in the stone,
In each creation, love is shown.

Time stands still, the world outside,
In this haven, dreams abide.
Whispers of the artisan's hand,
Create a magic, vast and grand.

Threads of Imagination

In a fabric woven with dreams,
Threads of thought unravel seams.
Colors shimmer, patterns swirl,
An endless dance, a vibrant whirl.

Each stitch tells a tale untold,
Of worlds unseen and treasures bold.
Fleeting visions twist and weave,
In the loom, they spin and cleave.

Fingers glide with gentle grace,
Creating realms in a sacred space.
A tapestry of hopes displayed,
In the light where dreams cascade.

Through woven paths the heart can roam,
In the fabric, we find our home.
Threads of gold and silver shine,
Crafting journeys, yours and mine.

Imagination's breath on high,
Lifting spirits toward the sky.
In the weaver's hands, we find,
A symphony of heart and mind.

Journey of the Dreamweaver

Beneath the stars, the dreamweaver flies,
Chasing whispers in velvet skies.
Stitching dreams with silver thread,
In the realm where none have tread.

With every note, a vision grows,
A dance of light, the cosmos flows.
Through starlit paths, the heart will chase,
Finding solace, finding space.

In the silence, stories breathe,
Moments captured, webs we weave.
Threads of hope that gently guide,
In the night where dreams reside.

A journey vast, with every turn,
Lessons learned, and candles burn.
The dreamweaver's touch is soft and light,
Transforming shadows into bright.

In the tapestry of night so wide,
The dreamer's soul cannot hide.
Journey onward, never cease,
In dreams, there lies our peace.

Sculpting Stars in the Void

In the cosmos, hands reach high,
Sculpting stars in the midnight sky.
From distant realms where shadows play,
Creation unfolds, night turns to day.

With each stroke, a constellation shines,
Carving light where darkness entwines.
Galaxies bloom in silent grace,
A dance of wonder in infinite space.

The void sings a lullaby sweet,
In the silence, hearts skip a beat.
Sculptors gather, weaving the night,
Fashioning dreams from sheer delight.

Stars above like jewels rare,
Twinkle softly, a secret affair.
In this stillness, we find our voice,
In crafting dreams, we make our choice.

Sculpting memories with every breath,
In the cosmos, we conquer death.
Shining bright, we forge our path,
Lost in wonder, found in math.

Color and Form in Motion

Vivid hues blend in a dance,
Shapes unfold, twirl, and prance.
Deep reds and bright blues sway,
A canvas alive, in bright display.

Every stroke tells a story,
A journey of fleeting glory.
Brushes glide with soft grace,
Capturing time in a fleeting space.

Sculpted shadows catch the light,
Figures emerge, bold and bright.
Textures echo soft to hard,
Artistry, an endless card.

In motion, the colors sing,
Form and rhythm, the heart's spring.
A symphony of sights to see,
Life expressed in harmony.

Each moment shifts, then resets,
Nature's palette never forgets.
Color and form, a boundless flight,
In the embrace of day and night.

Breath of the Universe

In silence, the cosmos breathes,
A vast expanse, the heart seethes.
Stars whisper secrets of old,
Galaxies in dreams unfold.

Each heartbeat resonates far,
Connecting here to where we are.
Time drifts softly, like a sigh,
Awakening the night sky.

Planets spin in cosmic waltz,
Gravity's dance, no faults.
Celestial bodies, they collide,
In a unison, all abide.

The universe hums an ancient tune,
Comets race, a fleeting boon.
In the dark, a spark ignites,
Illuminating endless nights.

With every breath, we are one,
Underneath the shining sun.
In every atom, life connects,
A symphony the cosmos reflects.

Symphony of Whispers

In the stillness of the night,
Soft whispers take their flight.
The breeze carries tales untold,
Secrets shared, gentle and bold.

Leaves rustle in rhythmic flow,
Nature's chorus, sweet and slow.
Echoes of laughter, faint yet clear,
A symphony that draws us near.

The moon hums a lullaby,
Stars twinkle, winking from high.
Creaking branches, a soft sigh,
Under the vast, endless sky.

Each moment a note in time,
Harmonies intertwine, sublime.
In quietude, the world spins,
Where silence and music begins.

Together we sway, hand in hand,
Treading softly on this land.
In the whispering night we find,
The symphony of heart and mind.

Labyrinths of Imagination

In the mind's eye, worlds expand,
Labyrinths built on shifting sand.
Winding paths of thought and dreams,
Reality bursts at the seams.

Creativity flows like a stream,
Fleeting glimpses of a dream.
Twists and turns, a playful chase,
Discovery in every space.

Ideas weave, a tapestry bright,
Fables born in eager flight.
Strange creatures in shadows roam,
In this maze, we find our home.

A realm where silence speaks loud,
And wonders gather, proud and shrouded.
Echoes of visions, wild and free,
In these labyrinths, we shall be.

So let your mind take to the skies,
In the heart of the maze, arise.
For imagination knows no bounds,
In its embrace, magic resounds.

The Architect's Odyssey

In shadows deep, he crafts his dreams,
Blueprints whisper of ancient schemes.
With every stone, a tale unfolds,
A journey grand, through time, he molds.

Against the sky, his towers rise,
Defying storms, they touch the skies.
Each arch, each beam, a story weaves,
Of hopes embraced, and time's reprieves.

Beneath his gaze, the city breathes,
In crowded streets, where life believes.
He shapes the space where hearts collide,
A haven where the lost confide.

With every bolt, he finds his way,
Mapping dreams to light the day.
Endless roads of steel and stone,
This architect, forever known.

His odyssey will never cease,
For in each line, there's boundless peace.
A legacy, of heart and mind,
In every structure, life entwined.

Navigating Uncharted Waters

The horizon stretches, far and wide,
With sails unfurled, the waves collide.
Stars above guide the path ahead,
In whispers soft, the ocean said.

Each swell a story, deep and vast,
Of sailors brave, who faced the blast.
Their voices echo in the night,
As dreams take flight with daring might.

A compass true, yet hearts may sway,
In currents strong, they lead astray.
But every storm brings lessons learned,
As lanterns far, the tide's returned.

With courage bold, they steer the course,
Through rolls and tosses, with steady force.
Each wave, a test, each gust, a call,
In uncharted waters, they won't fall.

Together bound, through trials great,
They find their peace, they find their fate.
In every splash, a truth they find,
To navigate the ties that bind.

The Symphony of Birth

In gentle hush, a new life sighs,
A melody beneath the skies.
With whispered dreams, the world awakes,
A fragile heart, as morning breaks.

From silence born, sweet cries emerge,
A symphony, where hopes converge.
Each note, a testament of grace,
In every smile, love finds its place.

As fingers grasp the air, so mild,
The universe bends for the child.
In eyes that shine, a story's told,
Of journeys vast, and dreams of gold.

Through tender hands, the world unfolds,
As laughter dances, their hearts behold.
In starlit nights, they find their way,
In the symphony of life, they play.

And as they grow, the world will see,
The song of hope, of bravery.
Bound by love, the music swirls,
A masterpiece, as life unfurls.

Molding the Ether

In quiet dusk, the spirits weave,
Threads of thoughts, they softly cleave.
Molding ether, where dreams reside,
In whispered winds, they seek to glide.

Ethereal hands transform the night,
With colors vast, they paint the light.
Creating worlds where visions flow,
In boundless space, their wonders grow.

Through layers deep, the essence beams,
A dance of shadows, a waltz of dreams.
With every pulse, a spark ignites,
In realms unknown, the heart invites.

They shape the stars with tender care,
In cosmic winds, their souls laid bare.
Uniting realms of thought and being,
In a tapestry of dreamland seeing.

As echoes fade, the ether hums,
In silence pure, the mystery comes.
For in this space, where dreams take flight,
They mold the ether, crafting light.

Forge of Possibilities

In the heart of the flame, dreams are born,
Ideas collide, creating forms unknown.
With each strike of the hammer, futures ignite,
A symphony of hope, in the darkest night.

Mold the raw essence of your desires,
Shape them with strength, the fervent fires.
Bend the metal of will with hands so sure,
Forge your path, let your spirit endure.

Whispers of courage dance in the air,
As molten thoughts pour, without a care.
The anvil of time waits for none to stand still,
Set forth your vision, ignite your will.

With every twist and turn, destiny calls,
In the workshop of fate, each echo enthralls.
Craft what you seek, let your heart be the guide,
In the forge of possibilities, dreams will abide.

So hammer away, let your passion run free,
In the glowing embers, find who you can be.
The forge is alive, with potential untamed,
In the heat of creation, you'll never be blamed.

Harmony in Chaos

In the whirlwind of life, find your beat,
Amongst the disarray, discover your seat.
Rhythms entwined in a turbulent dance,
Embrace the discord, seize every chance.

Colors collide, a beautiful mess,
Amidst the confusion, let your heart express.
Notes may clash, but a melody grows,
In the chaos we find how harmony flows.

Echoes of laughter, whispers of pain,
In dissonance, we learn to remain.
Together we rise, though chaos might reign,
In the tapestry woven, there's beauty in strain.

So welcome the storm, let it echo your soul,
In the dance of uncertainty, surrender control.
For within the tumult, lies a vibrant song,
A harmony found, where we all belong.

Embrace the tornado, the flickering light,
In the heart of the chaos, lies infinite might.
For together we stand, in the thunderous fight,
In the harmony of chaos, we'll take flight.

Alchemy of Shadows

In the depths of night, where silence dwells,
Whispers of darkness cast enigmatic spells.
Shapes shift and shimmer, figures emerge,
In the alchemy of shadows, dreams converge.

Mists of the past swirl and twine,
Turning lost echoes into forms divine.
From sorrow to strength, each shadow we weave,
Transmute the pain, find what we believe.

Black and white merge in the tapestry spun,
Every dark corner, a journey begun.
Crafting our stories from twilight's embrace,
In the alchemy of shadows, we find our grace.

With courage we tread, through the murky unknown,
In the depths of our fears, true strength is shown.
For every dark moment holds a lesson's light,
In the alchemy of shadows, we conquer the night.

So dance with the specters that haunt your past,
Transform their meaning, let memory last.
In the light of acceptance, let the shadows unfold,
In the alchemy of shadows, find treasures untold.

Reflections of the Mind

In the mirror of thought, what do you see?
Fragments of dreams, whispers of me.
Images shifting, like waves on the shore,
In reflections of mind, there's always more.

Each thought a ripple, each feeling a wave,
Unraveling stories, the heart learns to brave.
Thoughts intertwining like threads in a loom,
Creating a fabric from joy and from gloom.

The labyrinth of reason, a maze to explore,
Within each dark corner, there's knowledge in store.
Shadows may linger, but light breaks the bind,
Illuminating pathways in reflections of mind.

So pause for a moment, let silence prevail,
Listen to echoes, let intuition unveil.
In introspection, the truths start to unwind,
In reflections of mind, a treasure we find.

Embrace your inner world, let it lead the way,
For within every thought, there's a chance to sway.
In the mirror of self, let the journey unwind,
In the reflections of mind, seek what's refined.

Meditations on the Maker

In quiet hours, thoughts arise,
Whispers of creation's ties.
Hands that shape both clay and sky,
Breath of life, a soft reply.

Stars that shimmer, dreams that soar,
Each heartbeat leads to something more.
Nature speaks in silent tones,
Crafting beauty from the bones.

In shadows deep, the light is born,
From stillness, chaos is adorned.
Every failure, a lesson learned,
From ashes, bright new worlds are turned.

Time flows like a river wide,
Moments dance, we cannot hide.
In every pulse, the Maker glows,
Through art, the universe flows.

Creation is a sacred play,
A symphony both night and day.
With every brush, we touch the divine,
In every stroke, the stars align.

Reflections of the Infinite Artist

A canvas bare, awaiting grace,
Colors merge, find their place.
Dreams take shape in vibrant hue,
Vision vast, yet pure and true.

Each stroke whispers of the soul,
The artist's heart, a silent goal.
Fragments dance in time's embrace,
Crafting worlds we dare to trace.

In every line, a story spun,
Reflections of the moon and sun.
The infinite inspires the finite,
In shadowed corners, sparks of light.

Wisdom flows through hands so wise,
As beauty springs from whispered sighs.
In each creation, a fragment shines,
Echoing through the grand designs.

With every piece, a journey starts,
Catching the beats of countless hearts.
The artist's dance, a timeless quest,
To capture essence, and never rest.

Crafting Light from Darkness

In the void, a flicker glows,
From the depths, creation flows.
Wisps of thought, like candle flames,
Drawing forth the hidden names.

From silence, echoes boldly cry,
A tapestry where shadows lie.
In the dark, potential sleeps,
Awakening, vast promise keeps.

Through tangled paths, we seek the spark,
Guided by the gentle dark.
Crafting light to break the gloom,
From humble hearts, the visions bloom.

A balance found, the night and day,
In every end, a brand new way.
With every doubt, the courage swells,
In secrets whispered, magic dwells.

From ashes rise, the phoenix gleams,
In twilight's hands, we sculpt our dreams.
Light against the dark prevails,
Crafting hope through endless trails.

The Spiral of Invention

Ideas swirl like autumn leaves,
Chasing thoughts that time retrieves.
In every twist, a spark ignites,
Crafting futures, igniting nights.

Curiosity, a guiding force,
Through winding paths, we chart our course.
Invention sings in varied forms,
From stillness, chaos often warms.

Each question asked, a door ajar,
Unlocking realms both near and far.
A dance of minds, a brave ballet,
Breakthroughs found in bold display.

With patience clutched, the goal in sight,
Innovation weaves through every flight.
From simple tools to grand debate,
The spiral speaks, revealing fate.

In the heart of every quest,
Lies the spirit of the best.
Each spiral turn, a lesson earned,
Invention's fire is ever burned.

Alighting the Blank Page

A canvas waits, devoid of sound,
Whispers of dreams start to surround.
Ink flows like whispers in the night,
Crafting worlds, igniting light.

With each stroke, a story is born,
Echoes of hope, by passion worn.
The pen glides on, a gentle dance,
Transforming silence into chance.

Thoughts take shape, begin to soar,
A symphony of words to explore.
Each letter, a step towards the sky,
Stitching moments as they fly.

The heart beats loud, a steady tune,
In the quiet hush of the afternoon.
Shadows and light intertwine and play,
Alighting the blank page, come what may.

A final glance, the work complete,
A journey launched, a pulse, a beat.
With every word, a piece of me,
A story shared, forever free.

The Dance of Inspiration

In the stillness, ideas stir,
A gentle breeze creates a blur.
Thoughts collide in perfect time,
Spinning dreams in silent rhyme.

With each step, a spark ignites,
Illuminating darkened nights.
In rhythms soft, imaginations play,
Discovering magic along the way.

Ideas whirl like leaves in a gale,
Through valleys deep, they twist and trail.
A sonnet brewed from whispered tunes,
In the glow of silver moons.

From shadow's edge, ambitions rise,
Dancing freely under open skies.
The pulse of art, a grand display,
In the dance of inspiration, come what may.

With every turn, a vision takes flight,
Creating visions both bold and bright.
Lost in the music, minds aligned,
Inspiration found, hearts entwined.

Flickering Flames of Thought

A spark ignites in twilight's glow,
Flickering flames begin to flow.
Thoughts like embers swirl and rise,
Dancing softly beneath the skies.

Each flame a whisper of what could be,
Fleeting shadows, wild and free.
In the hearth of dreams, they sway,
Lighting paths, showing the way.

As the fire crackles, ideas entwine,
Creating patterns, so divine.
A gentle warmth spreads through the air,
Fueling visions for those who dare.

Embracing chaos, sparks ignite,
Fading darkness, bringing light.
In flickering flames, thoughts converge,
An artist's heart begins to surge.

From the ashes, creation blooms,
In vibrant colors, love consumes.
Flickering flames, a beacon bright,
Illuminating the endless night.

Vistas of Vision

Beyond the hills, horizons gleam,
Unfolding dreams, a luminous beam.
Through valleys wide, the eye can roam,
In vistas of vision, we find our home.

Mountains rise with ancient grace,
A tapestry woven, time and space.
Each peak a promise, each path a chance,
Inviting all to join the dance.

In sunlit fields where shadows play,
We chase the dawn of a brand-new day.
Colors burst, the heart's delight,
In every dawn, there lies a fight.

Pouring over pages filled with dreams,
We navigate life's winding streams.
With every step, a new perspective,
In vistas of vision, we find collective.

No limits here, just sky and sea,
A journey shared, you and me.
Through scattered clouds, our spirits soar,
Vistas of vision, forevermore.

Horizon of Creation

At dawn the world awakens slow,
Colors drip from skies aglow.
The light unfolds, a canvas wide,
With whispers of the stars inside.

Mountains rise like ancient lore,
Guardians of the dreams in store.
Rivers hum a soft refrain,
Carrying tales through sun and rain.

In fields of gold, the shadows play,
Dancing lightly, fading gray.
Each petal tells a story grand,
Written in the softest sand.

Creativity flows from the heart,
A tapestry, each thread a part.
In every seed, the future sown,
From silent roots, new life is grown.

The horizon beckons, bright and clear,
A promise held, for all who steer.
Join the journey, seek the light,
In this creation, take your flight.

Odyssey of the Dreamweaver

In twilight's grasp, the dreams take flight,
A tapestry spun from starlit night.
Whispers of wishes weave through the air,
The Dreamweaver dances without a care.

With threads of silver, and shadows deep,
She crafts the visions that softly creep.
Each heartbeat a promise, each sigh a song,
In the realm where the dreamers belong.

Through veils of time, she journeys wide,
Finding solace in the waves of tide.
Mountains fade into a hazy mist,
As realms of wonder through twilight twist.

With eyes like gems, she seeks the lost,
In every turn, she counts the cost.
Yet hope remains in every thread spun,
An odyssey shared, two hearts become one.

So dreamers gather, hear the call,
Under the roof where illusions fall.
In the embrace of night's cool grace,
Dance with the stars, join the chase.

Fragments of Infinity

Shattered pieces, scattered light,
Each a story held in sight.
Moments captured, glimmers bold,
In fragments, truths of life unfold.

The past echoes in whispered tones,
While future calls with unknown stones.
A puzzle unfurls, each piece aligns,
In the silence where the heart defines.

Through the void, a spark ignites,
Guiding souls through endless nights.
In every shard, a chance to find,
The hidden joys that life designed.

Boundless patterns, colors blend,
In every heartbeat, journeys send.
The dance of time in vivid hues,
In fragments collected, we choose.

With open hearts, we reach and grasp,
The threads of infinity softly clasp.
Each fragment shines, a radiant glow,
In this cosmic tapestry, we flow.

Nectar of the Soul

Sweet elixir, pure and bright,
Bottled dreams in the pale twilight.
With every drop, a story brews,
Of laughter shared and whispers to muse.

In gardens where the wild winds play,
The nectar flows, in sun's warm sway.
Petals unfold like secrets told,
Rich in beauty, soft as gold.

Savor the sweetness, cherish the grace,
For in each moment, we find our place.
Time drips gently, a honeyed stream,
Filling hearts with love's pure gleam.

The soul awakens, dances free,
In harmony with the melody.
With each breath, the nectar flows,
A sacred bond, the spirit knows.

So gather 'round, let laughter swell,
Share in the tales each heart can tell.
In the nectar of the soul, we unite,
In the embrace of love's soft light.

The Art of Possibility

In gardens of thought, seeds are sown,
Color blooms where dreams have grown.
A canvas wide, the future bright,
Each choice a spark in the endless night.

Between the lines of doubt and grace,
Miracles hide, time can't erase.
With every step, a path unfolds,
New stories written, new tales told.

Whispers of hope in the quiet air,
Bridges to build, treasures to share.
Bold hearts ignite, passions flame,
In the art of us, nothing's the same.

Life's brush strokes, vivid and free,
Painted dreams on reality's sea.
Bold strokes challenge the status quo,
With courage, we rise, and boldly go.

Every moment, a chance to start,
Crafting futures, a world apart.
In the art of possibility's embrace,
We find ourselves in this endless space.

Echoes of the Unseen

In shadows deep where secrets dwell,
Echoes whisper, their stories swell.
Unseen spirits in twilight roam,
Weaving tales of a distant home.

Beneath the stars, a flicker glows,
A gentle guide where darkness flows.
The heart listens, though silence stands,
Unspoken words from ancient lands.

Mirrored reflections in moonlit streams,
Fragments of truth in our quiet dreams.
They linger on, a soft caress,
In twilight's grip, we find our rest.

Voices linger in the quiet night,
Calling forth like a beacon light.
In every crack, in every seam,
Resides the pulse of a living dream.

Those unseen threads that tie us near,
Binding hearts with love and fear.
In echoes deep, we hear the call,
The tapestry of life, our all.

Weaving Whims and Wonders

In looms of thought, we spin our dreams,
Fleeting moments catch the beams.
Whimsical threads of laughter bright,
Braid together through day and night.

Fables dance in the morning light,
Casting spells with colors bright.
Wonder drips like honey sweet,
Binding us in a rhythmic beat.

From merry tales to stories bold,
The fabric speaks of lives retold.
Each stitch a heartbeat, alive and clear,
In the web of time, we persevere.

Adventure waits in every seam,
A place where shadows dare to dream.
Wonders await with open hands,
In woven worlds, our spirit stands.

Let imaginations swirl and glide,
On whims of fate, we take a ride.
With every thread that we entwine,
In the tapestry of life, we shine.

Light and Shadow's Dance

In twilight's embrace, the two unite,
Light and shadow blend in flight.
A waltz of contrast, soft and stark,
Painting stories deep and dark.

With flickers bright, the shadows play,
Chasing dreams that drift away.
Every moment, a brief romance,
In luminous whispers, they take their chance.

Daylight molds the forms we see,
While night enfolds what's meant to be.
Together they spin, a timeless trance,
In the dance of fate, we take our stance.

They weave through time, each turn refined,
With every heartbeat, gently aligned.
From dawn's soft glow to dusk's caress,
In light and shadow, we find our rest.

Forever bound in a subtle sway,
In the art of being, come what may.
Through the dance of balance, we find our way,
In light and shadow's endless play.

Choreography of Creation

In the quiet glow of dawn,
Whispers dance and swirl around.
Nature breathes, its limbs extend,
A tapestry of life unbound.

With colors bright, the world awakes,
Each petal sways with grace anew.
Breezes sing, the branches sway,
Iyi symphony from every hue.

Mountains rise, they touch the sky,
Rivers flow with ancient tales.
Creation spins its endless web,
In harmony, the universe exhales.

Stars above, they waltz in time,
Moonlit shadows gently glide.
A choreography divine unfolds,
In every heart, creation resides.

From the stars to grains of sand,
Each moment, a spark of light.
In this dance, we find our place,
A creation born from night.

A cycle vast, yet beautifully small,
The world's embrace, an endless flow.
In every step, we share the beat,
The choreography of all we know.

Kaleidoscope of New Beginnings

In a world of fractured dreams,
Colors meld and come alive.
Each moment shifts, a vibrant scheme,
In stillness, new hopes thrive.

Morning breaks with shades of gold,
Promises painted on the sky.
Through shadows deep, our hearts unfold,
A kaleidoscope, we learn to fly.

Paths diverge and intertwine,
Choices echo in the light.
In every glance, a spark divine,
Painting futures, bold and bright.

With open minds, we venture forth,
Unlocking doors, breaking chains.
Each step, a testament of worth,
In the dance, joy remains.

Together we weave this tapestry,
Every thread, a story told.
In the depths of unity,
New beginnings flourish bold.

So hold on tight to what you seek,
Let your spirit guide the way.
In the kaleidoscope, we speak,
Of dreams that greet the day.

Embers of Innovation

From ashes rise the brightest sparks,
In shadows, ideas ignite.
With fervent hearts and daring marks,
We chase the dawn, embrace the night.

In the jungle of the mind,
Where chaos breeds creativity,
Innovation plays, unconfined,
As visions weave through infinity.

A fire starts with just a breath,
Flickering thoughts take their flight.
Against the odds, we conquer death,
Embers glow, relentless light.

In artists' hands, in thinkers' dreams,
New worlds unfold beneath our gaze.
Through trial's forge, imagination gleams,
In every heart, innovation stays.

Though failures linger, hope remains,
Each setback fuels a brighter tale.
In spark and flame, our courage gains,
Through storms of doubt, we shall not pale.

So let the embers rise anew,
A phoenix born from what once was.
In every heart, our spirit grew,
A dance of ideas, pure applause.

Pathways of the Mind's Eye

In whispers soft, the visions weave,
Paths unfold in twilight's glow.
The mind's eye sees what hearts believe,
In tangled dreams, we learn to flow.

Through forests deep and open skies,
Each thought a step along the trail.
Unfinished paths, where fortune lies,
In endless realms, we set our sail.

Fragments linger, memories call,
Each echo vibrant in the night.
The maze is vast, but we stand tall,
In the labyrinth, we chase the light.

With every choice, a new song starts,
Notes of hope, they intertwine.
In unity, our journey charts,
The beauty found in every line.

Through storms of doubt and valleys deep,
The mind's eye opens wide its door.
With steadfast faith, we dare to leap,
Exploring paths, forevermore.

In the dance of thoughts, we find our way,
A tapestry of life unfolds.
With courage strong, we seize the day,
In the mind's eye, our truth beholds.

Seeds of Tomorrow's Dreams

In the soil of hope we sow,
Tiny seeds begin to grow.
Through the dark and through the light,
Whispers tell of dreams in flight.

Gentle hands to tend and care,
Nurturing wishes, tender prayer.
With each sprout, a future glows,
In the garden, purpose flows.

Roots entwined beneath the earth,
Burgeoning with love and worth.
Dewdrops kiss the morning sun,
In this dance, our dreams begun.

Nature's chorus sings so sweet,
Every heartbeat feels the beat.
In the fields of what will be,
We plant our hopes, let them be free.

When the time is right to reap,
Harvest dreams that we shall keep.
In the twilight, shadows play,
Seeds of change will light the way.

Patterns of Whimsy

In the tapestry of night,
Colors blend with soft delight.
Shapes of laughter twist and twirl,
Each a fleeting, joyful whirl.

Dancing leaves in autumn's breeze,
Spinning stories with such ease.
Every moment, fleeting, bright,
Crafts a pattern, pure and light.

Whimsical dreams take their flight,
On the wings of stars so bright.
Echoes of a childlike heart,
In this art, we each take part.

Clouds become a canvas wide,
Imagination as our guide.
With each stroke of vibrant hue,
Crafting visions, old yet new.

Chasing shadows in the sun,
Finding joy in what we've spun.
Life is but a playful jest,
In the patterns, we are blessed.

Crafting Visions from Void

From the silence, thoughts emerge,
Born from absence, they converge.
In the void, possibilities,
Crafting dreams through subtle breeze.

Whispers float on fragile air,
Blueprints drawn with utmost care.
Every heartbeat shapes the scene,
Imagination, bright and keen.

Forms take shape in cosmic dance,
In the stillness, find your chance.
Mapping stars with eyes so wide,
Visions sparkle, like the tide.

Pages turn in endless quest,
Within the void, we find our best.
Creating worlds from atoms small,
In this canvas, we stand tall.

Dreams are woven, threads divine,
In the dark, our spirits shine.
Crafting visions ever bold,
From the void, our dreams unfold.

Whirlwinds of Thought

In the tempest, ideas swirl,
Like a dance, they spin and twirl.
Thoughts collide in vibrant clash,
Creating sparks in joyful flash.

Whirlwinds bring a rush of light,
Thoughts take wing, take sudden flight.
In the chaos lies the spark,
Illuminating paths through dark.

Every notion, wild and free,
Weaving threads of mystery.
In the storm, a clarity,
Whirlwinds shape our destiny.

With each gust, new visions rise,
Painting truths across the skies.
In the whirls of what we think,
Ideas flow, forever link.

So let the whirlwind spin and sway,
In the tempest, find your way.
For in the chaos, wisdom brews,
Whirlwinds gift us vibrant views.

Mosaic of Thought

In fragments bright, ideas blend,
A tapestry where dreams ascend.
Colors splash on canvas wide,
Each notion's spark, a joyful guide.

Whispers of the mind take flight,
In every shade, a glimpse of light.
Patterns dance, a story woven,
Through pathways clear, the truths are proven.

Wonders born from distant lands,
Connecting more than fate commands.
A swirl of voices, hearts ablaze,
In unity, our spirits raise.

Reflections deep in every gaze,
A harmony that gently plays.
In silence found, the echoes ring,
A choir of thoughts, together sing.

So cherish well each fleeting thought,
A mosaic bright that can't be bought.
Life's beauty rests in every part,
A cherished map of every heart.

Celestial Threads

Stars are stitched in velvet night,
Glimmers born from ancient light.
Each constellation tells a tale,
Of journeys vast that hearts unveil.

Comets blaze with fiery grace,
In the cosmos, they leave no trace.
Infinite dreams within our reach,
Galaxies whisper, wisdom teach.

Planets turn, their paths entwined,
In this dance, our fates are lined.
Orbiting hopes, we strive to find,
A universe that speaks to mind.

Beneath the moon, in soft embrace,
We ponder time and endless space.
Threads of fate connect us all,
A tapestry on love's great wall.

Let every heartbeat raise a prayer,
To the heavens, bright and rare.
In cosmic wonder, we shall dwell,
With celestial threads, we weave our spell.

Breaths of the Universe

In every sigh, the cosmos swirls,
A rhythm deep, as time unfurls.
Galaxies pulse with a knowing beat,
In this dance, our souls do meet.

Whispers carried on winds so pure,
In nature's grasp, we find the cure.
Each moment's breath, a gift of grace,
In the silence, we find our place.

Stars exhale their radiant light,
Guiding dreams through the velvet night.
The universe hums a lullaby,
Awakening wonder as we fly.

In every heartbeat, life renews,
A sacred bond that intertwines the hues.
With every star, a wish is cast,
An echo of futures, rooted in the past.

So breathe it in, this cosmic air,
Feel the warmth, it's everywhere.
In every breath, the universe sings,
A symphony made of all living things.

Radiant Pathways

Along the trails where shadows play,
Light emerges to greet the day.
Every step, a story shared,
In radiant glow, all hearts declared.

Sunrise paints the world anew,
With colors bright, a vibrant view.
Each path we walk, both bold and true,
Unfolds a journey meant for you.

Branches whisper, winds compose,
In nature's arms, the spirit grows.
The light will guide through darkest hours,
In every soul, a field of flowers.

Together we explore each bend,
With open hearts, where dreams ascend.
In luminous threads, our lives entwine,
Creating bonds that brightly shine.

So take a step, let the light ignite,
Radiant pathways, pure delight.
With every heartbeat, embrace the chance,
To dance through life, a joyful prance.

Blueprint of Existence

In shadows deep, the figures roam,
Life's design, a cosmic tome.
Threads of fate intertwine and weave,
In silent echoes, we believe.

Stars align in patterns grand,
Whispers guide, a steady hand.
Every heartbeat tells a tale,
In this journey, we prevail.

Colors splash on canvas wide,
Painting dreams we cannot hide.
In every stroke, a life is born,
From dusk till dawn, the world is worn.

Time moves softly, carrying grace,
In every moment, we find our place.
Blueprints forged in love and light,
This existence, a splendid flight.

Together we rise, together we fall,
Bound by the rhythm, in unity, we call.
Through storms we sail, on waves of bliss,
In the blueprint of life, a divine kiss.

Trail of Creation

From dust to stars, the journey flows,
Trail of creation, where wonder grows.
Seeds of thought in fertile grounds,
Nature's secrets whisper sounds.

Each breath a spark, igniting the fire,
A dance of dreams that will not tire.
Carved in whispers, the moments unfold,
Stories of life in colors bold.

We walk the path, with echoes near,
Memories linger, crystal clear.
A tapestry woven with threads of time,
In every heartbeat, we hear the chime.

Through valleys low and mountains high,
Kites of hope soar in the sky.
Every gesture, a stroke of fate,
The trail of creation, we celebrate.

With open hearts and minds set free,
We paint the world in harmony.
In the journey of life, we find our role,
A path of creation, nourishing the soul.

Crafting the Cosmos

In the workshop of silence, stars ignite,
Crafting the cosmos, a wondrous sight.
Galaxies swirl in a celestial dance,
Weaving together fate and chance.

With stardust fields and moons made bright,
Artists of time create with delight.
Each planet spins in perfect grace,
In this grand tale, we find our place.

The whispers of space call out to the wise,
Tales of creation beneath vast skies.
From chaos sprung, a harmony sings,
In the tapestry of life, hope springs.

Threads of light in the fabric vast,
Embracing the future while honoring the past.
A cosmic symphony played through the years,
In every note, we hold our fears.

Crafting the cosmos, hand in hand,
Together we rise, together we stand.
In the stillness, let dreams intertwine,
As we shape the stars with love's design.

Symphony of the Unseen

In quiet whispers, the world breathes slow,
A symphony of the unseen, aglow.
Notes of nature, soft and sweet,
In every heartbeat, life's pulse beats.

The dance of shadows beneath the moon,
Melodies rise, a soulful tune.
Within silence, stories unravel,
Paths we tread, the dreams we travel.

Harmony flows through branches and streams,
Echoes of laughter, fragments of dreams.
In every silence, secrets unfold,
A symphony waiting to be told.

With open ears, we heed the call,
Whispers of love that transcend all.
In the unseen, beauty we find,
A world united, hearts intertwined.

So let us listen, let voices blend,
In the symphony of life, we transcend.
Guided by music, through shadows we gleam,
Together, we weave the tapestry of dream.

Luminary's Odyssey

In the dark, the stars do gleam,
Guiding dreams through night's soft seam.
Across the cosmos, a path unfolds,
Stories whispered, adventures untold.

Winds of change in the silence blow,
A step, a leap, into the glow.
With every pulse of the brightening light,
Hope ignites the endless night.

Echoes of worlds that came before,
Each heartbeat opens another door.
The journey dances, swift and free,
A cosmic bridge to eternity.

Carried forth by dreams sublime,
We chase the spark, we chase the rhyme.
Together we wander, relentless and bold,
On a quest where stories unfold.

And when the dawn breaks over the sea,
The luminary waits, awaiting thee.
With eyes alight and spirits bright,
We embrace the day, bathed in light.

Crafting Whimsy

In a world of colors, bold and bright,
We weave our dreams in morning light.
With laughter's thread and joy's embrace,
We dance through time in endless grace.

A sprinkle of magic, a dash of cheer,
We pen the tales that all hold dear.
From clouds of cotton to skies of blue,
Our hearts create, our minds pursue.

With playful strokes upon the page,
We break the molds, we free the cage.
Each word a brush, each thought a hue,
Crafting whimsy as we construe.

In lantern lit nights, our stories soar,
With endless laughter, we explore.
A symphony in every glance,
Join the frolic, take a chance.

As light fades softly, dreams do gleam,
In whimsical realms, we chase the dream.
With hearts as canvases, love's refrain,
We build our world, we break the chain.

Dance of the Innovator

In the glow of morning, visions arise,
Where thoughts take flight and ideas surprise.
Step by step, we navigate the maze,
Unraveling wonders, igniting the craze.

With nimble feet on the edge of change,
We wander forth, seeking the strange.
Each motion a spark, each glance a cue,
In the dance of creation, we find what's true.

From sketches of dreams to bricks of gold,
We forge ahead, brave and bold.
Shaping the future with every design,
In rhythm with time, our spirits align.

As twilight beckons, shadows play,
Ideas flicker, night turns to day.
In the heart of creation, we move with flair,
Dancing the path of those who dare.

With hands entwined, we sculpt what's new,
Through trials and triumphs, we find our view.
As the world spins, we weave the thread,
In the dance of the innovator, dreams are fed.

Illumination's Footsteps

Through valleys deep where shadows lie,
A flicker glows, a gentle sigh.
In quiet corners, the light takes form,
Illuminating hearts through every storm.

With every step, a pathway shines,
Guiding souls through tangled vines.
In whispers soft, the truth is found,
In illumination, we are unbound.

The echoes call to those who roam,
In search of warmth, in search of home.
With every heartbeat, brightness grows,
Unveiling secrets the darkness knows.

Step into the radiance, embrace the glow,
Together we rise, together we flow.
With footsteps echoing on the ground,
In illumination, joy is found.

As sunsets paint the sky with grace,
We find the love in every space.
In the light of hope, we stand so tall,
For in illumination, we conquer all.

Fountains of Inspiration

In quiet moments, thoughts arise,
From depths within, where wisdom lies.
Whispers of dreams, like rivers flow,
Igniting hearts, they start to glow.

Each drop of hope, a spark of light,
Guiding souls through the darkest night.
With every wave, a new chance blooms,
Creating art in silent rooms.

In nature's breath, we find our muse,
Painting visions in vibrant hues.
A dance of colors, wild and free,
Unlocking secrets, just for me.

The echoes linger, soft and sweet,
In the space where two worlds meet.
Fountains splash with creative bliss,
Inspiring hearts to dream and kiss.

So let the waters flow and gleam,
Ignite the world with every dream.
For in each trickle, life confides,
A tale of hope that never hides.

Fragments of a Lost Dream

In the shadows of the night,
Whispers dance, just out of sight.
Fragments floating, lost in air,
Remnants of a beauty rare.

Once a vision, clear and bright,
Now a ghost in fading light.
Scattered pieces, hearts forlorn,
In the silence, dreams are born.

Memories weave a tapestry,
A bittersweet melody.
Time's embrace, both cruel and kind,
Leaves us searching, lost, resigned.

Yet in the chaos, hope is found,
In every sigh, a softer sound.
Rekindling sparks of what has been,
Transcending places we've not seen.

So here's to dreams that softly rise,
Over valleys, beneath the skies.
Though lost, they linger, never fade,
In the heart, their echo played.

Journeys through the Soul's Canvas

On the canvas of our lives,
Each stroke tells the tale that thrives.
Colors bright and shadows deep,
Secrets hidden, thoughts to keep.

Wandering paths, both rough and smooth,
Each step a chance, a gentle groove.
Textures blend in vibrant hue,
Reflecting dreams both old and new.

With each heartbeat, art ignites,
A dance of shadow, a flash of light.
Journeys carved through every thought,
In the silence, battles fought.

Brush the edges, feel the pain,
On this canvas, joy and strain.
Every crack, a story weaves,
In every tear, the spirit breathes.

So take a moment, pause and see,
The art of life, a grand decree.
Through every journey, paint your soul,
In strokes of love, we find our whole.

Building Bridges with Sparks

From heart to heart, we forge a way,
With kindness woven in the fray.
Building bridges, strong and wide,
Joining souls that once would hide.

In the silence, sparks ignite,
Connecting dreams in shared delight.
With every laugh, a bond is sealed,
In the warmth, our fate revealed.

Through storms we stand, hand in hand,
In unity, we make our stand.
Mending rifts with gentle grace,
Finding hope in every face.

So let us gather, rich and poor,
Unlocking every closing door.
With love as light, we pave the way,
Building bridges every day.

Together we rise; together we soar,
In the harmony, we yearn for more.
With every spark, a dream ignites,
Creating futures, chasing lights.

Footprints of Innovation

In the quiet of the night, a spark flies,
Dreams take form beneath starry skies.
Ideas dance like shadows on the ground,
Footprints of change in silence are found.

New paths forged with every whispered thought,
A vision of futures, unbought, uncaught.
With courage to leap, they venture forth,
Innovators rise, giving birth to worth.

Through trials and errors, they brave the storm,
Each failure a lesson, each loss a new form.
Carving our future with every step made,
In the hall of progress, their dreams cascade.

The world awakens to their loud cries,
Transforming the present with brighter ties.
The footprints they leave are paths to explore,
An echo of greatness that opens the door.

In every heartbeat, the heartbeat of change,
Inventive souls that feel the wide range.
The pulse of tomorrow, alive and strong,
In the footprints of innovation, we all belong.

Conductor of Fate

In the orchestra of time, a baton waves,
Life's notes rise and fall, like the tides and graves.
With each motion, fate finds its way,
Guiding the rhythms of night and day.

A conductor stands, arms open wide,
Invitations to dreams where shadows hide.
Melodies weave through the fabric of trust,
Each moment, a chord, in destiny's gust.

In harmony's grip, we dance and sway,
Following the score that the stars convey.
With precision, time unfolds its embrace,
Each heartbeat aligned in our rightful place.

The silence between holds its own weight,
Awaiting the cue, a prelude of fate.
Every life a symphony, rich and profound,
Creating a tapestry, joyfully bound.

Interpret the silence, the whispers so clear,
For the conductor of fate always draws near.
With each passing note, in the realm of chance,
Life's opera unfolds in a grand, timeless dance.

Dawning Realities

As dawn breaks bright, new light appears,
Chasing away the remnants of fears.
The crisp air sings with a vibrant hue,
Awakening dreams in a world made anew.

With every sunrise, possibilities bloom,
Casting aside the shadows of gloom.
A canvas unfurls with each waking breath,
Painting our lives, defying the death.

Hope spills over like rivers of gold,
Each moment a story waiting to be told.
With every heartbeat, realities form,
As aspirations rise, defying the norm.

In the glow of morning, we find our way,
Navigating paths where shadows may sway.
With courage ignited, we step to the light,
Embracing the dawn, igniting our fight.

As day unfolds, our spirits ignite,
Chasing the dreams that spring from the night.
In the dawning realities that greet our eyes,
We find the strength where true courage lies.

Labyrinth of Inspiration

In the maze of thought, where echoes dwell,
Whispers of genius begin to swell.
Every corner turned reveals a new spark,
A labyrinth woven in shadows and dark.

Paths intertwine in a dance so divine,
Where each twist and turn unearths a line.
A cacophony of voices beckons us near,
Inspiring the wanderers, dissolving the fear.

The walls are adorned with stories untold,
A treasure trove waiting, amidst dreams bold.
Through cracks in the surface, a wisdom flows,
In each shared journey, the heart truly knows.

With each step we take, new visions arise,
Secrets of passion hide in disguise.
Navigating the turns, we find our own song,
In the labyrinth of inspiration, we all belong.

So chase the unknown, let curiosity lead,
For in every exploration, there lies a seed.
A chance to create, to learn and to play,
In the heart of this maze, we forge our own way.

Shadows of the Muse

In twilight's embrace, whispers entwine,
Each flicker of thought, a thread in the line.
Dreams swirl like dust, in abandoned halls,
Where echoes of passion softly calls.

A canvas of night, where stars dare to peek,
With shadows that dance, and secrets they speak.
In the realm of the heart, creativity flows,
As the muse, in silence, ever glows.

With every stroke bold, the darkness ignites,
In the silence, we find our own flights.
Through struggles and joys, the spirit will rise,
To capture the light, hidden in the skies.

In the shadows we find, not fear, but the grace,
Of journeys within, that time can't erase.
A sanctuary built from fragments of dreams,
Shadows of thoughts, where the heart truly gleams.

And when morning breaks, the veil gently tears,
With visions unbound, igniting our cares.
The muse leads us forth, where heartbeats collide,
In shadows we wander, together, as guide.

The Infinite Playground

Beneath the vast sky, children at play,
In fields of wonder, they chase dreams away.
With laughter like music, they dance through time,
Creating their worlds, each moment a rhyme.

The swings touch the clouds, the slides sparkle bright,
As imagination takes off in flight.
From castles of sand to seashells of lore,
They build and they break, yet always want more.

In the whisper of trees, they hear stories told,
Of bravery, friendship, and treasures of gold.
Their hearts open wide, like petals in spring,
In the infinite playground, they find joy to bring.

With painted skies blue, and sunflowers bold,
They craft their adventures, both timid and bold.
Every laugh shared a memory, gold-threaded,
In this realm of freedom, where dreams are all fed.

As dusk paints the horizon, their journey won't cease,
For in every child's heart, lies infinite peace.
And though they may grow, their essence remains,
In the playground of dreams, love forever reigns.

Radiance of Ideas

In the quiet of thought, a spark starts to glow,
Ideas like fireflies dance in the flow.
Bright visions unfold, illuminating the night,
Bringing forth brilliance, a wondrous sight.

With whispers of wisdom, we find our way,
Through tangled pathways where shadows may play.
Each concept a seed, in fertile ground sown,
Blossoming gently, until brightly grown.

The tapestry woven with threads of the mind,
Creates a mosaic, unique and refined.
In clusters of thoughts, like stars in the skies,
They shimmer and shine with unlimited ties.

Through challenges faced, innovation takes flight,
Transforming the dark into shimmering light.
Ideas, like rivers, will flow and expand,
Connecting each heart, forging futures so grand.

As tools in our hands, we mold and we shape,
The radiance shining, each vision escape.
For in every glimmer that breaks through the haze,
Lies the power of change, to uplift and amaze.

Harmonizing the Cosmic Symphony

In the depths of the night, stars hum a tune,
A symphony soft, beneath the bright moon.
Galaxies swirling in rhythmic embrace,
Each note a reminder, we're part of this space.

From whispers of comets to planets that spin,
The cosmos resounds with the stories within.
Celestial melodies echo from afar,
Uniting the universe, each light, every star.

Through the vastness of time, the music resounds,
In the heart of the silence, true beauty abounds.
Symphonies woven with threads of the night,
Awakening spirits, igniting our flight.

Each heartbeat a rhythm, each soul a refrain,
In the dance of existence, we lessen the pain.
As harmonies blend in a cosmic delight,
Together we sing in the glow of the night.

So let the stars guide us on this grand stage,
Where each note of love turns the cosmic page.
In the symphony's heart, we find our own song,
In harmonized joy, where all beings belong.